# I CHOOSE
# to Say No

OSE
SERIES

ELIZABETH
ESTRADA

# I CHOOSE
# to Say No

ELIZABETH ESTRADA

I like to receive hugs,
Especially when I'm feeling blue.
Showing compassion is nice,
And something we can do.

But there are times a hug or touch
Is not something I want or need.
And it's not cool to force me to hug back,
Unless I've agreed.

My body is mine,
And I have a choice who I let near.
If I don't feel comfortable,
Then I just say, "No," to be clear.

If someone wants to hug me,
And I don't want to,
I just say, "Let's fist bump,"
Or "No, thank you".

There are plenty of moments in my life
That I look around and I feel safe,
Like when I'm around my Circle of Trust,
That's when I have the most faith.

My Circle of Trust is made up of several adults
Who I know I can turn to.
If a person has touched me inappropriately,
I tell them because they'll know what to do.

Like when I'm reading books at bedtime,
And my parents are tucking me in tight,
I feel confident and happy,
As they go ahead and turn out the light.

There are other times I don't feel safe,
When my Circle of Trust are not near,
When someone is touching me
And I suddenly feel fear.

I am aware of any Early Warning Signs
And how to look for danger.
I am especially cautious
If I am ever talked to or touched by a stranger.

My Early Warning Signs are when my heart beats fast
Or my breathing slows down.
Sometimes my Early Warning Signs means my head gets dizzy
And spins around and around.

I can feel my Early Warning Signs
At anytime, anywhere.
Especially when members
Of my Trusted Circle are not there.

I call my private parts by their real names
Like vagina and penis,
When I know the names of my body parts,
It helps me explain any abuse.

If someone talks about my private parts,
I know what I should do.
I tell someone in my Circle of Trust
Or an adult at school.

I choose to say no
Because my body is mine to control,
Feeling safe, calm, and protected
Is always my ultimate goal.

Saying no is up to me
And it's nice to have a choice,
To have a say over my own body
And to clearly use my voice.

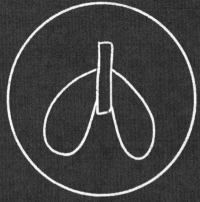

## Early Warning Signs
- Hands shake
- Heart beats fast
- Head gets dizzy
- Breathing slows down

# Circle of Trust

Please write the names of people who belong in your Circle of Trust.

Made in United States
North Haven, CT
10 September 2022